The NOT So Special Fish

Written by Eissa Albinali

Illustrated by Paola Acosta

Copyright © 2023 Eissa Albinali

All rights reserved.

To my dear mother, who not only taught me how to swim against the current, but also showed me the beauty of forging my own path.

In a vibrant coral reef lived a little fish, surrounded by lively and colorful creatures.

Yet, this little fish felt out of place among his peers, as his scales were dull and gray compared to the dazzling hues of his friends.

One of his friends was brilliantly orange and blue, reminiscent of a tropical sunset.

Another swam with the grace and speed of a silver dolphin.

Yet another possessed the strength of a shark.

Within his heart, the little fish couldn't help but feel a twinge of envy as he gazed at his friends, yearning to be as bold and striking as they were.

He confided in his mother, saying, "Mama, why am I not as colorful, fast a swimmer, or as strong as my friends?"

Mama smiled and replied, "Well, my little one, maybe you should try eating more of the biomolecules."

"Biomolecules?" the young fish asked, "Will eating them make me more colorful, faster, and stronger?"

"Eating them will make you the most colorful, fastest, and strongest little fish in the entire coral reef," Mama said with a twinkle in her eye.

The little fish had never heard of these mysterious biomolecules before and eagerly asked, "Which foods have the most biomolecules? I want to be the most colorful, fastest, and strongest fish in the coral reef."

Mama explained that biomolecules are found in all the foods we eat and that there are three main types: carbohydrates, lipids, and proteins.

She gave the little fish a piece of bread, rich in carbohydrates, for him to chomp on. He took a bite and felt his energy levels rise.

Next, Mama gave him a slice of avocado, high in lipids, for him to taste. He took a bite and felt his swimming abilities improve.

Finally, Mama gave him a handful of beans, packed with protein, for him to try. He took a bite and felt his muscles grow stronger.

His speed increased, and he could swim all around his coral reef in record time.

The young fish's scales began to shimmer and sparkle with new colors, as if he were a kaleidoscope.

Finally, his strength grew, and he could carry the largest rock in the ocean with ease.

The little fish was overjoyed; he had become the most colorful, fastest, and strongest fish in the entire coral reef, just as his mother had promised.

Glossary

Coral reef:

A vibrant underwater garden. It's made of many small creatures called corals, which build beautiful shapes that protect and house all kinds of fish and sea critters. Coral reefs are like the neighborhoods of the sea.

Biomolecules:

Chemical building blocks that make up everything alive. Our bodies put biomolecules to work in order for us to function.

Carbohydrates:

Our body's main source of energy. They give us the fuel to run, play, and think.

Lipids:

They store energy for later use when we might need it. Think of them as little backpacks full of energy that our body can use whenever we're out of fuel.

Protein:

Our body's construction workers. They help build and repair things in our body, like muscles and skin. Imagine them as tiny workers in hard hats, busy making sure everything stays strong and in good shape.